THERE'S NO SUCH THING AS COINCIDENCE

By

Jan Wolterman

Pat –
Celebrate your life with God's love!
Jan Wolterman

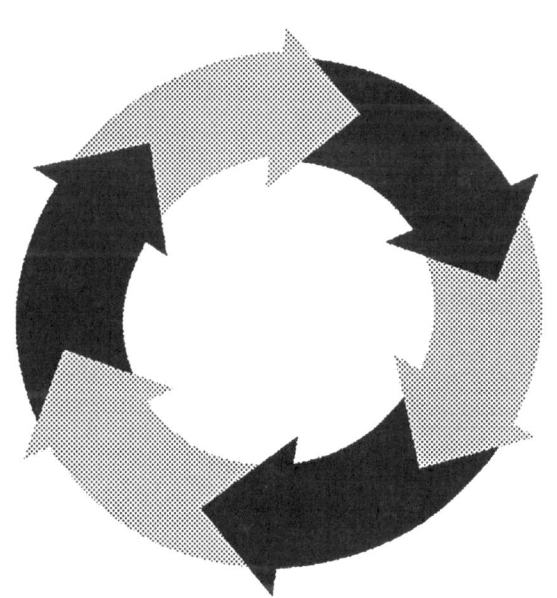

There's No Such Thing as Coincidence

Chapter One
Our Journey Through Life .... Page 5

Chapter Two
Love Story .... Page 15

Chapter Three
Good Stuff From God .... Page 28

Chapter Four
Good-Bye For Now .... Page 55

Chapter Five
You And Only You .... Page 66

Chapter Six
Workbook for the Soul .... Page 79

©1996 Jan C. Wolterman. All rights reserved under International and Pan-American Copyright Conventions. No part of this book may be reproduced without written permission from Universal Publications P.O. Box 53511 Cincinnati, Ohio 45253.

Chapter One

Our Journey Through Life

*God does not die on the day
when we cease to believe in a personal deity,
but we die on the day when our lives cease to be illuminated
by the steady radiance, renewed daily, of a wonder,
the source of which is beyond all reason.
---Dag Hammarskjöld*

In 1977 Father Mike was preparing for his vocation, living and studying at the old St. Mary's seminary located in Cincinnati, Ohio. He enjoyed his four years there and after becoming a chaplain for three local hospitals he would often return to St. Mary's to visit. Ministering to people who are suffering devastating illness and people who have lost loved ones is a demanding, stressful job so Father Mike relished an occasional 'escape' back to the seminary. He'd go up to his old room, number 148 on the second floor, to just sit, focus his thoughts and re-energize his soul.

In the summer of '95, he was making one such visit. By this time the seminary was not in use anymore. Father

Mike entered the deserted building, climbed the stairs and started down the hall to his room when his beeper went off. He carries a voice pager but the message being broadcast was so garbled he couldn't understand what was being said. Knowing full well it might be an emergency he immediately turned around, went back down the stairs, out to his car, and drove to a nearby gas station to use the pay phone.

After calling his staff at Providence Hospital he was told no, they hadn't paged him. The woman answering his next call to Children's Hospital also replied in the negative. Figuring it must have been St. Francis/St. George, Father Mike called his office there, only to hear his secretary say no, she hadn't beeped him either.

Concluding it must have been a wrong number, Father Mike headed back to the seminary. As he pulled into the parking lot he couldn't believe his eyes. In the eight minutes he was gone, the entire north wing, including room 148, had completely collapsed in on itself.

If you ask Father Mike who he thinks beeped him he'll reply, "I believe it was through the grace of the Blessed Virgin. St. Mary's was originally dedicated to her. Her promise to protect us from harm proved true."

Ask that same question, though, of a scientist or statistician and you'll hear answers like, "It was just someone who dialed the wrong number at the right time. It's a fluke. A coincidence, a pure chance occurrence."

Fluke or no fluke, Father Mike's life was obviously, remarkably spared by highly improbable yet highly significant circumstances. But why? How? And for what reason? This jovial man of the cloth laughs with his ready answer. "Either God isn't ready for me yet or he's afraid I'll take over in Hell."

Years ago I was driving through a subdivision with my dog on my lap. As I approached a three way stop, I slowed down and hastily glanced in all directions. I had every intention of sliding right through the intersection until my dog did something she'd never done before. She jumped out the car window, causing me to slam on my brakes in an abrupt halt. Before I could open my door to let her back in, a truck came flying out of nowhere to my right. I watched in horror as he ran his stop sign, then, unable to make the turn, demolished a mailbox on the opposite sidewalk. Had I breezed through the stop sign as intended, my dog and I would have been hit broadside by a speeding pickup.

These coincidences don't quite fit the definition Webster assigns it, events that come together without reason or an accidental occurrence of events at the same time. I don't believe Father Mike's beeper went off by chance nor do I believe my dog 'accidentally' jumped out my window to prevent an accident. Therefore, in this sense of the word, I don't believe there really is such a thing as coincidence. There's a reason for everything that happens in our world, doubly so for any coincidence.

Perhaps a better term to use is synchronicity, a word coined by the Swiss psychologist, Carl Jung. Synchronicity defines 'meaningful coincidence.' So throughout this book whether I refer to events as coincidence or synchronicity, I'm talking about incidents that have happened for a reason and have meaning.

So what exactly is this mysterious force that draws like and like together? It's baffled humans for eons and even today the experts don't agree on the answer. Scientists and others rub their hands in glee at the prospect of explaining these events away by using the law of averages or probability. This, however, doesn't mean coincidence can't have significance on several levels beyond statistical reality.

In some ways the metaphysical field and the scientific one are closely linked. Elmer Green, a pioneer with The Menninger Clinic in Alpha-Theta BrainWave Training States says, "It is interesting to note that a major concept of ancient metaphysical thinkers was that all matter is condensed energy, and that every piece of the cosmos (including the body, mind, and spirit of each human) exists in relationship to all else. In fact, the metaphysical concepts of energy and relationship in Tibetan Buddhism are remarkably similar to the energy and field theory of modern physics. In both systems it is hypothesized that one primary form of energy exists, from which everything else is constructed."

In many other aspects, science and metaphysics are worlds apart. Science accepts nothing as truth until it is subjected to comprehensive research and experiment with double blind studies and extensive laboratory testing. This works well for most subjects. It's extremely difficult though, to use these same tools to measure the ethereal effects of coincidental events.

One example of an experiment that raised more questions than could be answered was conducted by British scientists who rigged up a heat lamp so that it would turn itself on and off in an uncontrolled, utterly random fashion. Probability law predicts that, under these circumstances, the device will behave like a tossed coin. Runs of one outcome or the other can be expected, but in the long run the total minutes of off and on should be just about equal.

The scientists found the heat lamp conforming precisely to these predictions when it was sitting on a table by itself. However, when they placed baby chicks in an enclosure beneath it, the behavior of the heat lamp inexplicably changed.

The device remained on for longer times than it remained off. Was it due to the incessant chirping of the baby chicks who peeped miserably from the cold when the light went off? That's the only conclusion the scientists could reach. They think some order making force synchronized events in the chicks favor so that the light stayed on to keep the chicks warm. Just what this order making force is, they didn't say.

Synchronicity and other intangible subjects obviously don't pour themselves neatly into any mold of man's logic. Perhaps, therein, lies the problem. Logic is a human construct, a set of laws that seem to work very well for our purposes on Earth but may in fact have little to do with certain immutable laws of the Universe. It seems highly unlikely that humankind will ever identify the wrongness by applying more of the same wrong logic.

A revered yogi master, Sri Yukteswar stated, "All creation is governed by law. The principles that operate in the outer universe, discoverable by scientists, are called natural laws. But there are subtler laws that rule the hidden spiritual planes and the inner realm of consciousness; these principles are knowable through the science of yoga. It is not the physicist but the self-realized master who comprehends the true nature of matter. By such knowledge Christ was able to restore the servant's ear after it had been severed by one of the disciples."

Therefore the answer to the question of synchronicity varies, depending largely upon your belief system and how you view the totality of life. Perhaps I should say the explanations vary. Answer implies the solution to a problem and synchronicity isn't a problem to be solved. It's an experience to examine and an adventure to learn from in order to understand it's reason, purpose, and meaning.

The world of synchronicity makes more sense if we view ourselves as spiritual beings in a human body and not the other way around. Remember that your consciousness is holographic. This means that each unit of it has knowledge of the whole. Whether you realize it or not, your soul, encased in your spiritual body, contains information about the entire universe.

"Belief is more important than knowledge," said Albert Einstein. Having reasoned faith, not blind faith, in our convictions, is crucial in answering questions we have about our world. To have faith is to know you have a power within you that is always available. This power is what fuels synchronicity. I've noticed when one's faith increases, usually so do helpful 'coincidental' events.

One interesting concurrence happened to me while researching this book. I had just plopped down on the couch, early one afternoon, to watch a televised documentary when the electricity went out. About ten minutes later the phone rang. My college age son, Jim, was calling from school. His Professor had sent the class home that day with an essay question, part of their final exam, to be turned in the following morning. Jim was searching for answers to the question of why there is evil in a world of God and love. After some discussion of possible theories and explanations we hung up.

Since the television was still off due to the power outage I picked up a book I had obtained from the library that morning. As I slipped into a chair, the book on my lap fell open to a chapter titled, of all things, "Why There is Evil in God's World." I skimmed through its content then immediately called my son back to tell him what I had found.

"Great!" he replied. "Fax me that chapter!"

By now, about twenty minutes had passed since the loss of electricity. Amused, I reflected on what had just happened.

"Okay God," I jokingly said out loud. "I see now, one reason, why the electricity went out. You can turn it back on."

What could I do but laugh when, within one minute, the TV and lights all came back to life.

Sometimes, in order to come to terms with certain

enigmas of life, you just have to take the high road. The road from the eye to the heart that doesn't go through the intellect.

The British archbishop, William Temple, once remarked, "When I pray, coincidences start to happen. When I don't pray, they don't happen."

Unfortunately, some people simply aren't aware of their connection to God. Sadder still is the fact that even more of us aren't aware of our connection to one another. Synchronicity/coincidence makes us aware of both, along with being a subtle reminder we belong to a greater whole than the sum of our individual lives.

In regards to why synchronicity happens, whether we realize it or not, all the paths of our underlying consciousness connect with a universal all-knowingness. This provides an invisible link with all other souls. Hence the scene is set for inevitable, meaningful, inter-action to happen between us and others. Synchronicity usually happens when we need it. In a way it's as though our life spirit performs these mini-miracles in order to take care of our physically housed soul.

In the school of life, in which we're all enrolled, it seems any tests the Universe throws our way are like essay questions, with each of us writing our own autobiography as the answer. And in writing that story we are characters in many different plots and we travel many different roads; some planned, some unplanned, but all paths of learning and knowledge.

Hopefully, somewhere along that human path we'll encounter a spiritual awakening. In a letter Carl Jung wrote to Bill Wilson, the co-founder of AA, he stated, "The sole right and legitimate way to a spiritual awakening can happen only when you walk on a path which leads you to higher understanding. You might be led to that goal by an act of grace or through personal and honest contact with friends, or through a higher education of the mind beyond the confines of mere rationalism."

It is my hope this book serves as an inspiration for you to fully explore your own personal path. In the following chapters, as you read more about the intriguing and amazing synchronistic events that have happened to other people, be aware you too can open up your life to more 'meaningful coincidence'. It's simply a matter of recognizing the power within.

Ever notice how birds use their wings to soar to new heights? All of us, too, have wings. It's called our soul. And once we tap into its power and unconditionally open up our personal line to God, it will lift us higher than any bird could ever hope to fly.

Chapter Two
Love Story

Love is the emblem of eternity;
it confounds all notion of time,
effaces all memory of a beginning,
all fear of an end.

--- Madame de Stael

Do you realize the average person can move to any city in the United States and odds are in their favor they'll find someone there to fall in love with and marry? While this doesn't guarantee they'll reach the happily ever after part, it does prove Eros love, the kind that puts stars in our eyes and butterflies in our stomach, can be found everywhere.

This is a frightening, yet comforting, proposition. It's frightening if we believe there's one and only one person in the world who's perfect for us. How on earth, if there's so many conceivable partners, will we ever ferret out our soul mate, the one we're meant to travel through life with? It's comforting though if we don't buy the concept of soul mates, the idea of there being only one person out there who perfectly fits the other half of our soul. When we feel complete within ourselves we don't need to desperately search for our life partner. We know if it's meant to happen it will.

When it does happen it's quite often due to synchronicity. Coincidence seems to enjoy playing Cupid in bringing two people together. Especially through blind dates.

Herman's story will vouch for this. A story that was celebrated on the Oprah Winfrey show.

In 1944, interned at a concentration camp during Hitler's regime was a young man, fourteen years old, named Herman. Every day he would walk along the barbed wire fence, wondering if he had a future.

One day a young girl appeared on the other side. She asked Herman what he was doing in there.

Herman replied, "Can you give me something to eat?"

The girl took an apple from her jacket and threw it over to him. Thus began a friendship between the imprisoned lad and the young lady.

Every day she would bring an apple and a slice of bread for Herman to eat. One day Herman told her not to come back. He was being shipped to another camp.

Many years later, after the war, Herman moved to the United States. In 1957, a friend fixed him up on a blind date.

Herman says something seemed to draw him to this date and as they sat in his car talking, the woman asked him where he was during the war. When he said in a concentration camp, she replied she met a boy at one such camp and gave him some apples.

Herman said, "Over the fence?" As she nodded yes it suddenly hit him. "This boy, was he tall?"

She nodded yes again. "After a while, though, he told me not to come around anymore because he was leaving."

Herman cried out, "That boy was me!" He immediately proposed, saying, "You got away from me once but never again."

Synchronicity nudges us toward potential life partners then leaves us alone to exercise our free will in deciding whether or not to proceed with the relationship. It's like having the perfect mother who introduces you to attractive people then backs out of the picture.

Synchronicity can be sneaky too. Sometimes we think we're exerting control over our lives when in reality it's all an illusion. Jennifer discovered this the hard way.

Having just returned to work from a dental appointment, Jennifer, a buyer for a department store, sat at her desk thinking how much she hated blind dates. She had obliged well meaning friends by going out on two such dates in the past month and both had proved disastrous. Now, on a Friday afternoon, she unhappily faced spending another evening with a man she knew absolutely nothing about.

As the Novocain subsided and her gum began to throb, Jennifer's mood went from bad to vile. Her dentist had fitted her with a temporary cap to wear on a front tooth that was in the process of being crowned and she despised the way it looked. Concurrently she decided she also hated the way her social life was going. Impulsively she picked up the phone to cancel her date. After leaving a message on his answering machine that she was sick and couldn't go out, Jennifer suddenly felt much better. She was back in control of her life.

Soon after, her phone rang. It was a girlfriend, Phyllis, calling to invite her to a huge, singles, office party at a downtown hotel. Jennifer jumped at the chance. Now she figured she could start choosing her dates herself.

At the party, Jennifer and Phyllis were standing by the buffet, flirting with a group of guys, when Jennifer suddenly sneezed. She sneezed so hard the unthinkable happened. The temporary cap flew off her tooth. Jennifer watched helplessly as it shot under a nearby, food laden table. Though no one else saw the tooth fly, Jennifer was thoroughly embarrassed. Holding her hand over her mouth she quickly excused herself, then made a mad dash for the other side of the table. As nonchalantly as possible, she dropped to her hands and knees, lifted the tablecloth and crawled under. Her eyes, after much frantic searching, finally located the wayward crown.

Crawling toward it, Jennifer suddenly recoiled in horror as a male hand came from nowhere and grabbed the tooth. She looked up to find herself face to face with a waiter who had crawled in from the other side.

"Looking for this?" he laughed, dangling the temporary crown. Jennifer grimaced. "It's okay," he grinned. "I'm only masquerading as a waiter. Working my way through dental school. By the way, my name's Michael."

He handed over her tooth, holding her hand an extra second in the exchange. After slipping the crown back on, Jennifer smiled and relaxed enough to realize this waiter/dental student was not only charming but darn good looking too. They sat under the table talking. When Michael mentioned he was supposed to be out on a blind date with some 'babe' who had canceled on him, Jennifer laughed. She shyly replied she too was supposed to have gone on a blind date but figured the guy was a complete nerd so she had canceled also.

"Wait a minute," Michael demanded. "Your name isn't Jennifer Maloney, is it?" One look at her face and Michael knew. "So you're the babe and I'm the nerd."

They both collapsed in fits of giggles until interrupted

by Phyllis, who peered under the table, demanding to know just what was going on.

Michael and Jennifer eventually married and recently celebrated their tenth wedding anniversary.

Synchronicity bridges the gap between the conscious and the unconscious, between the world of mind and the world of objective events. As evidenced, it can vitally affect our lives. Too often though, we just shrug it off or give it mere lip service. If we stop and recognize this connection between the worlds of external events and inner experiences we find proof of reason and meaning in the chaos of the universe. We realize an inter-connectedness between all people; a current of energy that, like the hub of a wheel, has pathways which flow to and encircle the whole.

Synchronicity is more than just some theoretical idea. It serves as one of many roads to bring us into closer contact with our own consciousness and therefore with others. This consciousness is a combination of coherence and interaction as one with the world.

Sometimes synchronicity plays a role in bringing back together two people who should never have drifted apart.

Back before they were married, Scott and Marla had dated for a year and a half. They often talked about their future together and were very much in love. Or so they thought.

Stress in Scott's business and petty differences between them soon built up a wall of animosity and they broke up. Though both were miserable dating others neither one of them would break down and make the call for reconciliation.

Several months passed, months during which they neither spoke to nor saw one another.

One Spring day Scott's friends invited him to go with them to a Paul Simon concert to be held at a local university. Unbeknownst to them, Marla's friends had invited her to go to the very same concert.

Walking into the fieldhouse that evening, Scott, searching for his reserved seat, started down a long row. His heart jumped as his and Marla's favorite song, *Crazy Love*, began playing. Continuing across the row, he suddenly looked up to see none other than Marla, searching for her seat in the same row, heading directly toward him. Ten feet away their eyes locked. Without reservation they rushed into each others arms.

Out of 15,000 seats Cupid had wisely decided to place theirs side by side.

Synchronicity exists on all levels. It's interesting to note that in scientific experiments, when individual heart cells are placed in a petri dish, each cell contracts independently.

When several cells are added they fall in synch with one another and begin to beat with the normal, collective pulse of a healthy whole heart.

Some people experience small coincidences that nevertheless leave them feeling quite satisfied.

Dwight and Clarice went out to a steak house to celebrate their 36th wedding anniversary. As they walked in the front door of the restaurant they encountered their best man, who they hadn't seen in many years. Clarice enjoyed letting him know what they were celebrating because, she smugly told me, "This is the same man who predicted our marriage wouldn't last six months."

Parental love, so different from romantic love, is just as powerful a catalyst in triggering coincidence when it's needed. Joan A. experienced this.

Joan married a Japanese-American and because they were unable to have children of their own they adopted their first child from Korea, a beautiful little girl they named LeeAnn.

In 1969 they desperately wanted to adopt a second child but because Joan's husband was forty-five years of age, Catholic Charities wouldn't even talk to them about adoption because they felt he was too old. On a hunch, Joan called the local Children's Home and was connected with the head mistress. As she outlined her situation and explained they were most interested in adopting an Asian child, Joan heard the woman gasp. It seemed in the twenty years the mistress had been director at the home, only one Asian child was ever available for adoption. It was a Chinese boy who just happened to have been born the week before.

Joan and her husband became the proud parents of Jason, an adorable baby brother for LeeAnn.

It shouldn't be surprising that in this day and age the computer is proving to be a source of synchronistic energy as well. Love at first (web) site happened to Joe and Julie.

Julie, a registered nurse, and Joe, an airline reservationist, tried to conceive a child for three years. Having no luck, the young couple applied to an international agency, Americans for International Aid and Adoption.

One evening in January '96, during the snowstorm of the century, Julie decided to go to bed early. Her husband Joe, couldn't sleep and began playing on his computer. Scrolling through pictures of available babies at a web site maintained by Precious in HIS Sight, a private photo listing adoption service based in Waco, Texas, one small face jumped out at him. Joe remembers looking at that beautiful little face and feeling he was looking at his son. He quickly roused Julie out of bed and immediately, upon seeing the little boy, Julie agreed. They both felt this baby was meant to be theirs.

The next morning Julie called the agency. Because they had already filed their application they had an edge. The boy was quickly promised to them. One month later they flew to Seoul, South Korea, and within three days returned with their son, appropriately nicknamed *God's Will* by Julie's mother.

Joe and Julie feel blessed that everything fell in place for them. They realize if Joe hadn't been playing on his computer, the little boy could have been snapped up by another couple. And even though he was listed by the same international adoption agency they had already applied to, they likely would not have been contacted about him because he has a cleft lip and a cleft palate. They didn't realize they had written, inadvertently, on the adoption application that they would take a baby with a cleft lip *or* a cleft palate which would have left this little guy out because he has both.

While the arrival of a child into a family can be heralded by synchronicity, so too can their departure. Many people, upon losing a child, experience supernatural circumstances that leave them with feelings of peace and serenity regarding their loved ones passing from this world to the next.

A friend of mine lost her young daughter to a

misdiagnosed heart ailment. The child died suddenly, late at night, in the hospital. The mother went home, among grief and tears, and prayed for a sign that her daughter was somehow, somewhere, still alive. The next morning, before word of the child's death had spread, the mother opened her front door to find a large bouquet of daisies, her daughter's favorite flower, on her front porch, laid there as though they had been freshly picked from the meadow next door. Except it was the dead of winter and the meadow next door was blanketed in snow.

The 'coincidental' appearance of these daisies provided the mother with renewed faith and strength to go on.

Synchronicity often plays a pivotal role in rebuilding shattered lives. The following story is an apt illustration of this.

Jeff was a charmer. He was full of caring for others, even at the tender age of eleven. This budding artist, the oldest boy of Bonnie and Ron Long, especially enjoyed drawing heart shapes. Jeff always drew them in a distinct way with an arrow through the middle. Each Valentine's Day he would delight in gifting his parents with an elaborate, heart-covered, hand crafted card.

On January 25th, 1984, Jeff suffered an accident resulting in extensive head injuries. After agonizing time spent in the intensive care unit he was declared brain dead. Knowing Jeff would concur with their decision, the parents sadly agreed to donate his vital organs.

One cold, dry day in the week following the funeral, Bonnie, Ron and Jeff's maternal grandparents visited his grave. As they stood solemnly together in silence they suddenly felt as though heaven had directly opened up. Four perfectly shaped oblong pieces of ice floated down to earth, one landing in front of each of them. Bonnie quickly scooped hers up, marveling at its perfect fit as it lay nestled in her hand. The astonished group looked around for the source of these 'gifts', perhaps an airplane flying overhead or ice dropping from the branch of a nearby tree. Their search proved futile but their hearts slowly filled with an unexplainable peace and joy.

That summer, Bonnie and Ron took their children to Cedar Point Lake and Amusement Park. As the kids enjoyed the rides, the parents felt the need to be by themselves. The anguish of Jeff's passing still clouded their thoughts daily and so they took off for a walk on the beach.

Usually law abiding citizens, the young mother and father ignored two large NO TRESPASSING signs and headed down a secluded part of the beach. Though the lifeguard and security patrol were in clear view, no one said a word or attempted to stop them.

On they walked, over rocks and sand, driven by some unseen force, until they came to a fallen tree. Climbing on top of it, they looked down to see something that stopped them in their tracks. In the middle of the beach, with no footprints surrounding it, etched in the sand and embedded with pebbles, was a distinctly drawn heart with an arrow through it. Inside the heart were the words, *Jeff Loves You*.

There's obviously no earthly explanation as to how this heart in the sand appeared. Jeff's parents accept it as a beautiful, miraculous coincidence. A heavenly sign to Bonnie and Ron that Jeff is still very much alive, completely filled with God's love.

Chapter Three

Good Stuff from God

The only meaning life has is what we give it.
---Jaicee

Charlie Roth was the Admissions Director for a Northern Kentucky college. Frequently, to help with recruiting, he would take students from the college to various high schools. One such rainy evening found Mr. Roth and a bus load of college students hopelessly lost on the backroads of Kentucky. Rounding each bend, Charlie grew more and more frustrated. He had absolutely no idea where he was. With no gas stations or places to stop to ask for direction, he finally blurted out, "We definitely need to get some help here."

The kids on board decided to ask God for assistance and offered up some prayers; a method, Charlie, an agnostic, put little if any faith in.

A few minutes later, stopped at a crossroads, debating which way to turn, Mr. Roth watched as a large delivery truck rumbled past. On the side of the truck, in large letters, was the company logo and name. The logo was a large circular arrow pointing to the front of the truck with the company name, ROTH DELIVERY, in the middle. Charlie did a double take, then, at the student's urging, promptly turned left in the direction of the arrow. The teens howled with glee when, a few yards down, they spotted a sign for the 'lost' high school.

I know Charlie Roth. He's an extremely intelligent man with a keen, scientific mind. Logic, statistics, reasoning; these are the tools he uses to make sense of life. But they fell woefully short in helping him understand the above synchronistic event where God used a bit of humor to point him in the direction he should go while providing a meaningful boost of faith to the students aboard the bus. This is one experience where heart power, not brain power, sheds more understanding light on the subject.

When you look through a kaleidoscope, objects take on an amazing array of shapes and colors. You see ordinary things in an extraordinary way. This is what happens when we view life with a transcendent vision obtained through faith in God. It transfigures our experience. Looking deep within our hearts, tuning into our inner Self, we experience newfound meaning and obtain fresh perspectives on all life situations.

Life often doesn't seem fair. We are not all born equal in regards to health, economic status, or opportunity. We are however, all born equal in the image of God and we all have equal access to God. But because God gave man and woman free choice, each individual decides for themselves whether or not they want this divine relationship. We can choose to be seeds or rocks. The sun shines as bright on the seed in the soil as it does on a rock on the ground. The seed, however, basks in the light, soaks it up and uses it as energy to grow into a beautiful fruit, plant, tree, or flower. The rock, however, pretty much just sits there, changing little from year to year. You have the same choice. You can use God's love to transform your life and yourself and bloom where you're planted or you can choose to maneuver through life alone.

Tragedy doesn't discriminate. No one is immune from it. What determines its significance though is not the suffering itself but our reaction to it. The end result, the ultimate outcome, is really what matters.

Jake Plummer was able to turn tragedy into triumph when a devastating illness struck this young man in the prime of his life.

Jake loved airplanes and decided, at the age of ten, to

become a Navy fighter pilot. In 1981, after graduating with honors from the University of Cincinnati, he applied to the Navy aviation officer program at Pensacola, Florida. At six foot, five inches, he barely slipped under the height limitations but soon became an outstanding candidate.

Several months into the program Jake fell victim to a relatively unknown and devastating illness called Hemorrhagic Gastritis, a horrifying disease that usually kills it's victims within hours, from severe hemorrhaging of the stomach lining.

Navy surgeons battled valiantly to save Jake's life. They removed part of his intestines and all of his stomach. Jake spent the next six years in and out of various V.A. hospitals; classified as a 100% disabled gastric cripple with little chance for recovery. It was an extremely demoralizing situation, especially for someone so young, so energetic, and with such a brilliant mind. His future looked bleak.

One Spring day a nutrition specialist arrived at the V.A. to donate his services and state of the art knowledge. He designed a unique nutritional support system, enabling Jake to survive outside a hospital environment. Slowly gaining in strength and independence, Jake was determined to return to the Navy. Everyone, from V.A. doctors to Navy brass, advised him to forget it. It would just be impossible.

Impossible is not a word in Jake Plummer's

vocabulary. In 1987 Jake decided to petition the Secretary of the Navy, John Lehman, for reinstatement as an active duty Navy officer. There was really no way for Jake to perform this job physically but he was determined to make a comeback. Well aware of the mountains ahead he knew he had to start his journey with this small step of faith.

The odds were overwhelmingly against achieving an audience with Secretary Lehman, who would have to personally authorize Jake's request. Subordinates were sure to take the safe path and deny the request before it could climb very far up the chain of command. Jake knew he had to somehow contact the Secretary directly and so one wintery, Thursday afternoon, Jake's father wrote a pleading letter to Secretary Lehman. Enclosing Jake's reinstatement request, Mr. Plummer sent it with a prayer via Federal Express marked *Personal, Confidential,* and *Top Secret.* It was scheduled to reach the Secretary's office in the Pentagon by noon the next day.

The snowstorm caught even the weather forecasters by surprise. Over the mountains to the west of Washington, D.C., a blizzard came from out of nowhere and dumped over two feet of snow on the nation's capital early Friday morning. A half million commuters decided to stay snug in their homes, thanks to this un-anticipated cold blanket of white flakes.

Back in Cincinnati, Jake and his father were oblivious to the Washington weather. Mr. Plummer telephoned Secretary Lehman's office mid morning on Friday. The phone rang endlessly. Just as he was ready to hang up, someone answered. The lone security officer informed him there was no one in the office due to the blizzard. Jake and his father were devastated. They seemed to be literally, frozen out, in their attempt to reach the Secretary. But Mr. Plummer isn't one to give up that easy. He asked the security officer how he could be sure the important Federal Express letter he had sent had been received at all. After a long pause, the officer said he would transfer the call to the Pentagon's huge mailroom.

"Perhaps someone there made it in today."

After a second a voice came on the phone that sounded just like Granny from the Beverly Hillbillies television show. Her West Virginia accent was only secondary to her distinct air of authority.

"Hi, this is Loretta. What's on your mind?"

Mr. Plummer knew he'd have to explain quickly but was interrupted by Loretta after only a few sentences.

"No need to go on," she said. "I know exactly which letter you're askin' about cause I just finished readin' it."

"What?" gasped Mr. Plummer. "You just finished reading my confidential letter to the Secretary of the Navy?"

"You got that right, mister," Loretta continued. "Yes siree, I've been supervisor in this here Pentagon mailroom for almost twenty-five years and nothing, absolutely nothing, comes in here 'less I know 'bout it."

Mr. Plummer decided it best not to challenge her perceived role as censor of Pentagon mail, especially those marked personal and top-secret.

"Well, then," Mr. Plummer asked gently. "What do you think about my son's request, Loretta?"

"Lord, it sure sounds to me like Jake is someone who deserves a second chance after all he's been through. You know, we see a lot of big brass with chests full of medals 'round here. Do 'em some real good to help out one of the little people for a change, don't you think?" Before Mr. Plummer could say a word Loretta continued. "I am gonna make sure Secretary John Lehman personally reads your letter first thing Monday morning. And I do mean first thing. You see, ain't nobody 'round here mess with ole Loretta," she sputtered with a nasal twang. "No sireee - nobody."

Mr. Plummer was incredulous. "You can guarantee something like that?"

"Why honey, just consider it done. This here letter will be on the seat of his fancy red leather chair so he won't be able to ignore it. And there's not a secretary or assistant who will dare touch it 'cause they'll know who put it there." Her snarl carried an air of authority reserved only for power wielding career civil servants.

"Bless you, Miss Loretta," was all Mr. Plummer could say as he hung up the phone with tears in his eyes.

The rest, as they say, is history. Not only did Secretary Lehman read the letter but he took immediate action. The Department of the Navy flew Jake to Washington, D.C., where he was interviewed for positions with a variety of the government's top rated intelligence gathering operations. Jake only had to agree not to request active duty with the Navy. A deal he happily agreed to.

Today, thanks to persistence, determination, faith, a freak snowstorm and a kind woman from West Virginia, Jake serves as one of the United States government's top, outstanding intelligence officers.

It's a miracle, Jake says. One that he and his family celebrate, at Christmas, every year.

Jake discovered one of the secrets in overcoming misfortune. He knew he wasn't fighting his battle alone. God was on his side. Can you imagine a more powerful ally?

When nothing seems to be going right in your life and you feel like you've hit rock bottom; rejoice! You have no where to go but up. Put yourself in higher hands; call on

God's strength to pull you to your knees.

Belief and faith in God is tremendously empowering because it emboldens belief and faith in yourself. Your capacity to lift yourself off the ground and get on with your life is limited only by you. Once you make the decision to release your old baggage and move forward you put into action supernatural forces. Only by surrendering can you win the war. Remember though, as committed as God is to helping you, only you can take that first step. Step out in faith and watch miraculous coincidences occur.

Goethe said it best:

There is one elementary truth, the ignorance of which
kills countless ideas and splendid plans:
the moment one definitely commits oneself,
then Providence moves too.
All sorts of things occur to help one
that never otherwise would have occurred . . .
Whatever you can do, or dream you can do,
Begin it.
Boldness had genius, power, and magic in it.
Begin it now.

Paying attention to and being grateful for synchronistic events in ones life can lead to greater awareness of the power we have over our future in addition to realizing how interconnected we are to other people who share our universe.

Our fates are not pre-set in concrete. We are able to make choices every moment of every day that have negative or positive effects on who we are and how we live. Utilize and listen to your intuition and gut feeling when making these choices and you'll be amazed at how true your decisions then become.

Synchronistic events that save lives also tend to put the participants more in tune with God and the universe.

Ned H. is employed as a corporate pilot. In all the years he's flown, Ned had never turned down a flight request until one day in 1988. Feeling a sudden urge to finish some projects around the house, Ned decided, at the last minute, to take off work one Saturday in February.

The day proved uneventful until mid-afternoon when Ned was suddenly gripped with severe chest pressure and began sweating profusely. Having just passed his annual physical the day before with flying colors, Ned laid down, thinking it would pass. It didn't. His mind quickly switched gears as his thoughts flashed back to a television show he had watched just one week before. A show on cardiac arrest that highlighted all the symptoms he was now experiencing. He remembered the physician saying that if you get into a comfortable position and that doesn't bring relief you are probably having a heart attack and to get to a hospital. Fast. Which is exactly what Ned did.

Once there the doctor immediately administered a shot of TPA. The pain quickly subsided. This specific hospital had just started using this particular drug for heart attack and Ned was one of the first patients to receive it. After a week in the hospital Ned underwent quadruple by-pass surgery.

Ten months later, after extensive rehabilitation, on December 24th, Ned received his best Christmas present ever. In the mail that day was his renewed pilots license. Now, every six months, he undergoes comprehensive stress tests as precaution.

Ned and his wife Barbara, shudder to think what might have happened had Ned flown a plane that day of the attack. They're grateful not only for Ned's cosmic nudge to stay home but for the resulting lifestyle changes. From healthier eating and exercise habits to a newfound philosophy of living each day to the fullest, Ned and Barbara are thankful for their very healing synchronistic event.

Meaningful coincidence often dramatically changes people's lives. Paulette's experience not only changed her life but ultimately saved it.

Approaching the grand old age of forty, Paulette was tempted to write off her aches and pains to middle-age.

Besides, she had been to several doctors over the past year, searching for a diagnosis of her chest and shoulder pain but each, in turn, had a different remedy. One treated her for pleurisy, another thought it to be bronchitis, and so on and so on.

One morning in February, 1995, Paulette read in the Sunday newspaper about Hospice needing volunteers. The small blurb jumped out at her as she had often thought about volunteering but never quite seemed to get around to it. This morning, however, she felt compelled to call the number and so she picked up the telephone and dialed, leaving her name and phone number after the recorded message. Paulette never received a call back and forgot all about it until the following Sunday when she again read about another Hospice soliciting volunteers. This was a different chapter and with the urge now stronger than ever, she gave them a call the following business day. The woman who answered was enthusiastic about Paulette joining the organization and invited her to a training session to be held that week.

At the session Paulette listened with interest to the teacher explain patient procedures and what to expect. The nurse related a story about one patient, a mailman, who had pain in his shoulder for years but ignored it, thinking it was just caused by the stress of carrying his heavy mailbag. It turned out the man had developed cancer but the diagnosis came too late and he tragically died a premature death.

Paulette immediately associated this with the pain in her own shoulder and called her family doctor that afternoon to make an appointment for the next day. When she arrived at her physician's office she was dismayed to find the doctor had been called away on an emergency. Determined now, more than ever, to get to the bottom of her pain, Paulette resolutely took off for a medical center down the road. There the doctor gave her a complete exam and ordered extensive x-rays that were developed on site, a procedure unavailable at her doctor's office. The x-rays revealed a large mass in her chest. A mass that turned out to be lymphoma. Immediate surgery was followed by extensive radiation treatment.

Several months later tests showed the cancer to be in complete remission. Having been given this new lease on life Paulette celebrated that summer by marrying the man she loves.

It's truly amazing how God often places people in the right place at the right time to help others in need. Dr. Philippe Duc, an employee of Procter and Gamble Pharmaceuticals in France, came to Cincinnati on a two week business trip in March of '95.

One evening, a friend, Walter, called to invite Philippe

to a local Aikido club to watch a testing event. Having practiced Aikido for seven years, Philippe held a brown belt in the craft but declined Walter's invitation. He had already planned a quiet evening in his hotel to catch up on some reading. Shortly thereafter, Walter called again. After much cajoling Philippe finally agreed to go with him to the downtown Aikido club.

After a few hours of watching the test participants, Philippe and Walter decided to go get a bite to eat. As they were leaving they heard an alarming, loud thump. Turning back, they saw Tom, a 57 year old man who had been testing, collapsed on the mat. Rushing to his side, Dr. Duc tried to locate a pulse that was no longer there. Tom wasn't breathing and had no discernible heartbeat when Philippe started CPR. After several minutes of this life giving technique the man still gave no response. Relentlessly continuing the procedure, Philippe was soon joined by a nurse and ten minutes later, the paramedics. They immediately hooked Tom up to administer electric jolts to his heart muscle. The third shock did the trick and he was rushed to the waiting ambulance.

Later, at Christ Hospital, the doctors told Tom how lucky he was to have had a cardiologist at his side within seconds of his attack. Thanks to Philippe and a subsequent by-pass operation, Tom is now fully recovered and back to practicing Aikido.

People who make their living by doing God's work experience frequent synchronicity.

Bart Steever, Associate Minister of the Mt. Washington Church of Christ in Southwestern Ohio likes to quote this passage from the New Testament book of Hebrews, Chapter 13, verses 1 and 2. *Let brotherly love continue. Be not forgetful to entertain strangers: for thereby some have entertained angels unawares.*

After what happened to him, Bart thinks you can't be too careful when it comes to this 'angels unawares' thing. Especially around Christmas time.

Two weeks before Thanksgiving, a mixed group of twelve people, including lawyers, doctors, social workers, and even an undertaker, traveled to Haiti to construct a church building.

While waiting in the Miami airport to board their flight to Port Au Prince, a member was approached by a man attracted to the *Northwest Haiti Christian Mission* t-shirts the group was wearing. The man gave his name as Bob. He claimed to be representing a group of humanitarians who were looking to give $5,000 to an orphanage in Haiti. Apparently Bob had done some benevolent work with an orphanage in Somalia and now was looking for a mission a little closer to home.

Bob was directed to Diana Owen, a member of the group who just happened to know of such an orphanage. Larry and Diana Owen had been working as directors of the Northwest Haiti Christian Mission, based in Versailles, Kentucky, for the past seventeen years. Larry's compassion for children in Third World countries developed during a tour of duty as an MP in Vietnam. When he had to leave he vowed it would be the last time he ever abandoned a group of needy kids.

Driven by an intense devotion to their Christian faith, Larry and Diana had found the perfect place to invest their energies - the northwest territory of the island nation of Haiti. In seventeen years the mission had established churches, schools, nutritional/feeding programs, and closest to the Owen's heart, an orphanage in the town of Port au Paix.

The orphanage residence had a deteriorating roof that leaked worse with each rain storm. A month previous, Larry had gone ahead and ordered the materials to replace the roof. Having no mission money to cover the cost, Larry put it on his personal American Express card. Diana questioned the sanity of doing this (not the first time she's questioned his sanity, she says) but Larry felt he had no other choice. The bill totaled $4,000.00.

Back in Miami, Diana told Bob about the mission and he asked if he could tag along on their trip. Though everyone was somewhat skeptical about "Somali Bob," as he came to be known, he proved to be a genuine guy. He was not only non plussed by the 'truck ride from hell', an accurate description of the 8-12 hour drive between Port au Price and Haiti's north coast, but by the time they arrived Bob proved to be part of the team.

After visiting the orphanage the next day Bob reached into his pocket and pulled out a wad of bills. Pealing off $4,000 in hundreds he placed the cash in Diana's hand and said, "Here. Take this. This is the kind of situation we were looking for. Send me a picture of the roof when it's completed and I'll send you another $1,000." Soon after, he boarded a chartered aircraft to Port au Prince and was gone.

Bart Steever and his group sat around that night and had a long thought-provoking discussion about angels, miracles, and the crazy ways that God often answers prayer. They agreed that the more you hang around with God, the more amazing 'coincidence' you run into.

They eventually found out that 'Somali Bob' lives in Cape May, New Jersey, where he's a partner in a golf course. So his residence isn't in Heaven. At least, not yet.

Bella Briansky Kalter, a writer, experienced a serendipitous encounter on a trip to Israel in 1994. She and her family's visit to the city of Ra'anana coincided with a huge festival celebrating Israel's 46th anniversary.

Thousands of people were present and as Bella sat among them, her husband suddenly noticed a man nearby who was wearing a *Northern Serenity - Iroquois Falls, Canada*, sweatshirt. Since the Canadian town Bella grew up in, Ansonville, had been renamed Iroquois Falls, she curiously approached the gentleman. Their ensuing conversation revealed an amazing coincidence.

Not only did they grow up in the same town but Bella's father, Pinchas Briansky, had taught this man Hebrew and helped prepare him for his Bar Mitzvah.

It also turned out this man, Albert Abramson, usually carried a treasured news article with him, a story written for the American Jewish Archives about the vanished Jewish community of their home town of Ansonville. A story written by Bella Briansky Kalter.

This fortuitous reunion, highlighted by the spiraling fireworks from the city festival, reminded Bella of a poetry her father might have spoken as he looked up from the pages of the Torah. *There is no beginning and no end. What was is and always will be . . . if so you will it.*

There's an invisible bond between friends that often surfaces when one is searching for the other. That bond became visible for Rick and Diane C. of Olympia, Washington.

They had attended a draft horse event about six hours from their home and decided to head back earlier than planned so they could stop for dinner and hook up with some friends who lived in Seattle.

Arriving in the city, they were unable to remember their friends phone number and so called directory assistance. When the voice on the phone asked what city, Rick replied, "Seattle."

"Go ahead", said the operator.

"Could you give me the number of Marcy Anders?" Rick asked.

The operator hesitated a second. "Hey, is this Rick?"

Taken aback Rick slowly replied, "Well, yes. Who are you and how did you know that?"

The operator stated his name was Michael and explained they had met at Marcy's graduation party from art school. A slightly shocked Rick clarified why they were calling.

Michael laughed, "Hold on a sec and I'll find out if the Anders are free this evening because Marcy is walking by my desk right now!"

It turned out Marcy also worked at the phone company and had Rick and Diane called about twenty seconds later she would have answered the call herself.

Synchronicity gave me a helping hand recently in the preparation of a newsletter. My husband is one of sixteen children and so with over seventy people in the immediate family we publish a quarterly newsletter just for the fun of it.

One busy day I was heading out the door to make copies of and mail the latest edition when the phone rang. It was my husband calling for his sister Ali's phone number. I had just finished printing out an updated list of everyone's address and phone number to include with the newsletter and so coincidentally had the list right in my hand. As I scrolled down and found Ali's name I was startled to realize hers was the only one out of the whole group I had forgotten to add the phone number to. A case of synchronicity masquerading as proof-reader.

Ed Morgan, a veteran of WW II, experienced a remarkable event on a trip to Europe.

Ed had served in the United States Army as part of Infantry 104. One December day during the war he was sitting on the bank of the river Roer in Duren, Germany, waiting for the river to subside so his troop could cross and attack the Germans on the other side. The river was swollen because the Germans had blasted the dams up river in order to make the water impassable. Ed and his unit watched and waited for over three weeks until the river had subsided enough to cross. During this time Ed could see the German soldiers across the river, beyond a brick wall, marching solemnly up and down a trench.

The call finally came. The American Army unit crossed the river at three o'clock in the morning, scrambled up the opposite bank and clambered over the brick wall. Fighting was intense with many casualties.

Over forty years later, in 1985, Ed Morgan decided to re-visit Europe. Once there, he went to Germany to re-trace the path he had followed during the war.

When he visited the town of Duren he went down to the Roer river and was surprised to find how little had changed. The old creamery building they had used as their post was still erect and as Ed looked across the river he could see the brick wall still standing on the opposite bank. Beyond the wall small cottages had been built but other than that the place looked eerily the same.

Ed crossed the river, this time over a modern bridge, and walked back to the place where his platoon had made their landing. Sitting on the brick wall in contemplation, he didn't hear the stranger walk up beside him. Startled, he looked up to see an elderly German man watching him.

Ed smiled and pointing across the river, said in German, "I was an American soldier and I was here during the war."

The German soldier put his hand on his chest, stood tall, and replied proudly in English, "I, Jakob, was here too, with the 59th division."

They soon realized that Jakob, who lived in a nearby cottage, was one of the German soldiers Ed had crossed the river to attack. Now, forty some years later, they sat and talked as friends. As the two of them discussed the war Ed wondered out loud why the Americans never were able to locate the bunker the Germans had used during that battle. Jakob smiled and took his arm, guiding him to his nearby home. They both laughed as Jakob showed Ed the hidden bunker. It was an underground storage area that now served as Jakob's potato cellar.

Automobiles and travel seem to be a catalyst for coincidental events. From running into people you know when you're far from home to being saved from bodily harm in car accidents, synchronicity stands out as a consequential factor.

A good friend of mine, Rhonda Patrick, tells of the time her mother and uncle stopped to pick up a stranger on a country road. This was back in 1945, when picking up hitchhikers wasn't the dangerous practice it is today. As they continued driving, a violent thunderstorm kicked up. Suddenly the stranger in the back seat yelled for the car to stop. Astonished, Rhonda's uncle quickly pulled to the side of the road. Before he could turn to question the back seat driver's sanity, a brilliant flash of lightning sliced off a huge tree limb in front of them. The gigantic branch fell directly on the road ahead. Right where their car would have been had they not stopped.

Coincidence? Had the man simply given in to an intuitive urge to yell out or had Rhonda's uncle inadvertently picked up a guardian angel?

Arthur S. learned to listen to his intuition after his synchronistic event many years ago.

In the early 1950's, before all the freeways were built in this country, Arthur was driving to Detroit with a friend. Night had fallen and the tree-lined back road he was traveling was pitch black except for the narrow glare of the headlights.

Arthur was averaging speeds of 70 miles per hour when all of a sudden a strong feeling came over him; an inner urging to slow the car down. As he quickly took his foot off the accelerator his passenger shot him a questioning look. Arthur just shrugged but said nothing as he continued to slow up.

Directly ahead, a huge shadow suddenly appeared out of nowhere. Arthur slammed on his brakes. Luckily he was able to bring the car to a complete stop inches in front of an unmarked railroad crossing. Just as a flat car, with an Army tank on it, rolled across their path.

Synchronicity played a prominent role in the lives of two reporters from Channel Nine news in Cincinnati. Not only did it protect them from possible harm, it helped them win an Emmy for news reporting.

Glen Rogers was an alleged serial killer being hunted across the United States. Paul Schaefer, a reporter, and Chic Poppe, a videographer, obtained a scoop on the case when a cousin of Rogers agreed to their request for an interview. The cousin lived in the mountains outside of Richmond, Kentucky.

Anxious to get on the road that morning, Chic impatiently waited for Paul to finish up another story that had unexpectedly popped up. They finally hit the road, heading south, about an hour and a half behind schedule.

Upon arriving in Richmond they first stopped at the Kentucky State Police Post to check in. As they were heading out the door to interview the cousin, a call came in on the police 800 hotline that stopped Chic and Paul in their tracks. It was from the very woman they were heading out to interview. She frantically told them her cousin, Glen Rogers, was just now leaving her house and he was driving a stolen car. The same house Chic and Paul would now be at had they not been delayed earlier in the day.

The patrol immediately issued an all points bulletin and off they went, including Paul and Chic.

A state trooper, twenty miles away, finally spotted Rogers car careening down the freeway. Pulling beside him, the officer tried to run the alleged murderer off the road. Rogers threw a beer can at the officer, laughed, and took off.

The police cars Paul and Chic were trailing sped to the highway Rogers was heading down.

Setting up a roadblock, they used Paul's Channel Nine news car to block traffic going the opposite direction. Chic stood behind the police cars, camera rolling, as the officers leveled their shotguns and waited. They didn't have to wait long. Rogers car soon came flying down the road with four police cars hot on his tail. Rogers, however, wasn't about to let a roadblock stop him. Amid a hail of bullets he swerved around them, nearly crashing into the news car Paul was sitting in, swerved back to the highway and took off again.

Rogers now had a contingent of police cars behind him with Chic and Paul bringing up the rear. It was all they could do to keep up with the officers as they reached speeds up to

120 miles per hour.

Two and one half miles down the highway, Rogers finally lost control and crashed his stolen vehicle. The exclusive news footage shot by Chic Poppe, who was in the right place at the right time, was seen around the world.

Automobiles can easily turn into death machines. Anyone who's ever been in a wreck will attest to that. Actually, most every knows this but not everyone believes it. Particularly teen-agers. At least I didn't when I was eighteen.

Back in 1970 I was a year out of high school and had just purchased a brand-new Capri sports car. I was in my glory driving that little stick-shift around town, from work to college to play.

On a lark, one winter day in March, my boyfriend and I decided to drive to Indianapolis from Cincinnati. Jim, home on leave from Vietnam, took the wheel and away we sped. We were young, we were free and of course we weren't wearing our seat belts.

Heading back home on the freeway it began to snow. Jim asked in a taunting voice, "What if we wreck?"

I remember shrugging my shoulders with a carefree laugh as I flippantly answered, "What if we do?"

Well, of course we did. Driving too fast on a slick overpass the Capri went into a spin. We side-swiped the car next to us, bounced off a concrete guard, crossed over two lanes of traffic and careened off the highway, just missing a thirty foot drop off, to slam headfirst into the side of a cliff.

As soon as the world quit crashing around me, I slowly opened my eyes. Surprised to find myself still in one piece, I pushed open my door and ran around to help a dazed Jim from behind the crumpled steering wheel. We hobbled to a nearby rock and sat down.

When the county patrol arrived he was surprised to find us alert and okay. Taking one look at the totaled car he just shook his head and said he couldn't understand, at the speed we were traveling, why I didn't go through the windshield.

I knew why, but it was years before I told anyone. I distinctly remember, at the point of impact, feeling a huge, soft, transcendent barrier between my body and the windshield.

This was one instance where the loving hand of God had reached out, literally, to embrace and protect me from harm.

Chapter Four

Good-Bye For Now

Life is a great surprise.
I do not see why death should not be an even greater one.
--Vladimir Nabokov

My flight to Florida was getting ready to board and I was a nervous wreck. This business trip was only for two days, so why the feeling of gloom?

Hesitantly approaching the agent, I handed over my ticket and started down the ramp. Suddenly I froze, engulfed in a feeling of panic. My heart began to pound and my mouth went dry.

"You can't get on this airplane," a voice screamed in my head. "Get out. Get out NOW!"

I slowly backed out of the tunnel. When an assisting flight attendant asked me if I was okay, I mumbled something about changing my mind.

With my ego tucked between my legs I hightailed it to the nearest phone to call my husband to come pick me up. I was in tears, embarrassed and humiliated. What on earth was my problem and why couldn't I get on that plane?

It would obviously make for fascinating reading if I were to tell you the plane crashed and everyone died except me, because my intuition kept me from boarding it. That, thankfully, was not the case. What did crash that day though, was my central nervous system. I had experienced a full blown anxiety attack because I was subconsciously afraid of flying.

Fast forward fifteen years. I'm on a return flight to Cincinnati from Los Angeles. Air turbulence is bouncing us all over the sky. In the rear of the plane I sit, a picture of tranquility. Why the change?

Had I downed a few drinks this time before boarding or popped some tranquilizers? No. None of the above. Over the years I had simply come face to face with a revealing fact. It wasn't the flying I was afraid of. It was the prospect of dying; the ultimate loss of control. That powerful fear of death, of the unknown, was therefore controlling how I lived my life. Not until I came to terms with the reality of death and what it really means to die, was I able to fully start to live.

Actually, none of us are afraid of death, per se. Unless

you've had a near death experience, you have no first-hand proof of what truly happens when you die. How, therefore, can you be afraid of something you basically have no knowledge of? Our fear is more a fear of the unknown. And like many things in life, we fear death mainly because we don't understand it.

The physical manifestations of death are extremely disconcerting. The person we love is no longer a person as we define the term. They no longer think, talk, or walk beside us. Whatever life force existed in them has vanished from our sight and so we lay the body to rest, deep in the earth, and we cry over their grave.

Chi, the life force energy in everyone of us, is composed of matter. It can be neither created nor destroyed. Your soul, the very essence of who you are, cannot die. It is indestructible. When our time on Earth is complete, we move on to a new life in a different realm.

No one but God can explain why one person dies as a baby while another lives to old age. Every human born, though, comes to Earth for a special purpose, possessing special gifts. It may be an opportunity for individual soul growth and/or it may be for spiritual advancement of others.

Remember, endings are always followed by beginnings. A quick look around your world will give you concrete evidence of this.

Many people experience strange phenomena when a loved one dies but most of them are afraid to talk about what happened for fear of what others will think. We need to be more open with our experiences because they can lead the way to understanding and peace.

Synchronicity tends to happen most often when we need it and that need is strongest when death comes calling. Coincidence often awakens an awareness factor that helps provide for satisfying emotional closure when death is at hand.

Mike and Carol experienced just such a coincidence on a business trip to Kentucky.

In their marriage, Sunday night is always pizza night. No matter where they go, Mike and Carol always make a date to have pizza together on Sunday evenings.

On a weekend trip to Louisville several years ago, Mike and Carol were searching, one week-end, for a good pizza restaurant. The first place they tried was full, they couldn't get in. The next place they located was closed. Ready to give up and head home, Mike suddenly remembered his Uncle George telling him that if he was ever in Louisville he should eat at Mama Grisanti's. Carol looked up the address in the phone book and off they went.

Uncle George was Mike's favorite uncle. Though

Mike hadn't seen him in several years, since they lived in different states, he was often in Mike's thoughts, especially this past year because George had been diagnosed with cancer.

As Mike and Carol entered Mama Grisanti's and made their way to their booth they passed by the bar. Mike was startled to see a familiar face seated on one of the bar stools. It was Uncle George, oxygen tank at his side.

It turned out George, against the advice of his family, was determined to make one last sales trip for his company and was passing through Louisville on his way back home to Alabama.

They all embraced and sat down together for dinner and reunion. It turned out to be a wonderful evening, highlighted by reliving fond memories of years past.

George passed on a few months after this chance encounter which made Mike all the more grateful for their unexpected reunion.

Another strange coincidence happened to Marjorie F. regarding her older brother, Tom..

On an April day in 1971, her brother, at 41 years of age, was rushed to a hospital suffering from kidney failure. The physician told the family that Tom's only chance at life was a kidney transplant. His three sisters all volunteered to be tested first for compatibility.

The day before the test, Marjorie was in her backyard, upset at the possible dire outcome, when she suddenly felt as though the weight of the world had lifted from her shoulders. Looking up to the clouds, she saw a vision of her brother. Tom's face was sun-tanned, he had a white silk scarf around his neck and he was smiling from ear to ear. Her sadness melted away like an ice cube in the sun as she felt a tremendous surge of inner peace and serenity.

The next day, Marjorie was chosen as the nearest match and in July the transplant took place. After recuperating in intensive care she returned to a six bed ward. The first thing she remembers, after the operation, is a small boy, the grandson of another patient, offering her a snack from his can of Planters' peanuts.

Later that night, when the family stopped by after first visiting her brother, they related to Marjorie how Tom had been craving a Planters Peanut candy bar and had given them orders to bring him one the following day.

Tom subsequently enjoyed two good years of life but the prescribed drugs eventually began to cause damage to his heart.

In December, 1972, he thought some Florida sun would help and flew down to spend time with a sister in

Lakeland. By the time Tom headed home he was extremely weak. As his wife drove back to their house from the airport, Tom asked to stop by to see Marjorie.

When they arrived at her house, Marjorie went out to see Tom since it was difficult for him to get in and out of his car. As she approached the automobile Tom rolled his window down. Marjorie was jolted by his appearance. He had a dark sun tan, a white silk scarf around his neck and he was smiling from ear to ear.

Tom and family celebrated Christmas together and he was even able to give his daughter away in marriage. He passed over soon after, in January of 1973.

Marjorie felt great satisfaction in knowing she had given her brother two additional years of life. Years he lived to the fullest.

A pet is a cherished and important member of many families and only those who've experienced the unconditional love of an animal can understand the anguish felt at their loss.

Jaime, a Chihuahua/Terrier mix, came into our lives as a tiny puppy but soon established herself Queen of the house. My husband wasn't thrilled with her at first. He said if we got a dog why didn't we get a 'real' dog, a German Shepherd or a Rottweiler. Jaime, however, was not deterred by his indifference. She slowly worked her way into his heart though

I'm not sure exactly when.

Perhaps it was the time he watched all eight pounds of her flying low as she chased a huge deer across the yard. Or maybe it was the time she broke her leg tangling with a dog ten times her size who dared to trespass on our property. At any rate, they soon became inseparable buddies. So much so, that when he'd kiss me good-bye in the morning she'd growl menacingly until she received her good-bye too.

Jaime didn't like to be outside by herself. Whenever we'd let her out it wasn't long before she was right back at the door, scratching to get in.

Jim would always yell, "Who's there?" and Jaime would answer with her trademark woof of two short barks.

We knew, at thirteen years of age, Jaime wasn't feeling up to par but we didn't realize to what extent. One morning we awoke to find she was gone. We had sworn she was with us the night before, she always slept at the bottom of our bed and so we anxiously began an exhaustive search of the house and nearby woods.

Outside, just as the sun was rising, I heard my husband yell. He had found her. While walking the trail in a nearby grove of trees he said he heard her bark. Twice. He immediately veered off the path and pushed his way through ten feet of brush and briars to find her under a tree. Her little body was stiff and cold. Jaime had died hours before.

The synchronicity of hearing a dead dog bark, thus leading us to find her body, can surely be written off as a hallucination or imagined response to an emotional experience. You're free to make of it what you will. As for the two of us it was a magical moment filled with grace. The sun rose that morning to find two people embraced in tears of sorrow and tears of thankfulness, having been given the knowledge and assurance that life goes on. For all.

Motherhood is the most creative role God, the Producer, ever cast. It certainly isn't a role that's easy to play. I was one of the lucky ones. Were it available, my mom, Minerva Winall, would have garnered an Academy Award for Outstanding Mother each year of her life. Not only did we have a great mother-daughter relationship but she was also my best friend. Needless to say, when she suffered a stroke in her late sixties, I was devastated.

Mom's stroke didn't leave her paralyzed, though I would have preferred that to the damage it did do. The affliction caused extensive brain damage and aphasia, the inability to talk and/or respond when spoken to.

We were never quite sure just what was going on inside her head because she was unable to express her feelings and emotions. Her mind operated like that of a young child.

Since she was also incontinent and unable to be left alone, our roles reversed. I became the mother and she the child.

Ten years passed with my mother in this condition.

Mom suffered her final stroke in October of '94. When the hospital called to tell us she had died, I felt both sadness and relief. Sadness at letting her go, relief at her finally being released from the 'prison' of a body she could no longer use.

The next morning, as we drove to the funeral home to make the necessary arrangements, my father quietly related something that had happened the night before. Dad had been sitting alone in the dark in his living room after the hospital call. All of a sudden he said he could have sworn he heard Minerva talking to him, clear as a bell. When I excitedly asked what she said, he answered with a slight hesitation.

"As though she were sitting next to me, I heard your mother say - *It's beautiful up here.*"

How wonderful of my mom's spirit to make one last contact with her husband to tell him, in a voice now loud and strong, not to worry. She's in beautiful surroundings, she's whole, she's happy, and she's at peace in her new home.

Examine death in its true context and you remove much of the trepidation surrounding it. Death is certainly to be mourned but it is not to be feared. When you understand your Spirit, the very essence of who you are, will never die, you can see how much meaning and significance your actions in this life have.

Death is the end of your physical existence on Earth but it is no more the end of your life than your birth was the beginning of it. You existed as Spirit before you were born and you will continue to exist after your physical body takes its last breath.

Life on Earth is a time to experience who you really are and who you want to be. It's a time to recognize the undisputable fact that God loves each and every one of us, so very, very much.

Make the most of this wonderful opportunity. Tune in to your higher Self so that you can live each day with unsurpassed Joy.

Chapter Five

You And Only You

Don't compromise yourself. You're all you've got.
--- Janis Joplin

      It seems, from my personal observance, that people tend to live out their lives on one of three floors.

      Some people live in the basement. In a life sparsely furnished with values and ethics, existing only for thrills of the flesh, these people, for whatever reason, choose to believe only in man and/or woman. To them there is no such thing as God or Creator. They meander through life with little direction or purpose, completely out of touch with their own true feelings. Usually irresponsible in their words and actions, cellar dwellers find little meaning or purpose to life. They don't believe in an afterlife and so feel all their actions on

Earth go unaccounted for. 'Do what you want, the hell with everyone else' is their slogan.

Next are those living on the first floor. These people may or may not believe in a Universal Creator but they definitely feel life has purpose and meaning. Often more religious than spiritual, too many in this group allow their personal dogma and doctrine to justify alienation of others. It's as though they can't see the forest for the trees. In addition, some of those residing on the first floor tend to, unnecessarily, live their lives with unresolved feelings of guilt.

Finally, residing in the Luxury Suite, are individuals who have learned that time on earth is a magnificient opportunity to do things that serve their own highest purpose. These folks seem fully aware of the choices available to them, in thought, word, and deed, and endeavor to choose those that express and expose the best they can be, as human beings. People in the Luxury Suite possess an 'indescribable' inner peace and serenity. They put God first in their lives. Their actions, motivated purely by love, reflect an unshakeable faith.

Pretend you're cruising down the highway listening to songs on the radio. The farther you travel from home the tougher it becomes to clearly hear your favorite station. The music tends to fade in and out. If you keep driving, it eventually becomes difficult, if not impossible, to tune in at all.

So it is with life. The farther we stray from our home base, from tuning in to our inner Self, the tougher it is to play out our song. We also then tend to get stuck living in the basement or on the first floor when we could be enjoying all the benefits found in the Luxury Suite.

Oliver Wendell Holmes said, "The average person goes to the grave with his/her music still in them." Don't you owe it to yourself to fully compose and play out your life's ballad?

Life on Earth is a time for us to learn and remember what we already know for the continued growth of our soul. Whether you came into this world through love, lust, or rape, know there's a special purpose for which you were born. A unique reason and meaning to your being here. And in order to fully comprehend just what your role is, you need to tap in, and surrender to, the God within. Once you make this connection you open up your consciousness to all possibilities. Like a piece of thread weaving its way through the quilt of life, you connect with universal consciousness. This, in turn, opens up brand new pathways for coincidence/synchronicity to flow into your world. You will learn to love with your divine Self, to always expect the best as you graciously accept all the rest that is given to you. You will finally have arrived home.

Chartres Cathedral Maze

    The maze in the diagram above graphically illustrates this life process. It is a replica of a design on the floor of Chartres Cathedral in France. The center of the maze represents home as the center of yourself.

As you begin the puzzle, your journey to discover who you really are, home seems to be readily in sight. But as you follow all the twists and turns of the maze you find you have to cover a lot of territory before you're able to land in the center. So it is with our trying to figure out who we are, why we're here and what it's all about. We have to keep moving forward, keep discovering oneself, in this game of life. If we don't, we'll never arrive home and uncover the true reason and meaning we're here. And please don't say you'd rather not play because if you're alive, you're already in the game.

So exactly how do you go about finding yourself? Is there a magic password that allows one to open the door to that library of knowledge and wisdom inside all of us? Where can we purchase a sacred key that unlocks the Luxury Suite? How exactly do we find our internal compass that unfailingly points us in the right direction?

Basically, it comes from tuning in and listening to your inner voice, the voice of your higher Self that is in direct communion with God. It is the voice of Truth and it is the radar that steers your vehicle onto the right course to guide your journey.

One foolproof way to get in touch with your inner voice is through a comprehensive program of meditation and prayer. However, before delving into the specifics, a very critical point needs to be addressed.

The most important relationship you'll have in this life is with God, your creator. The second, and equally important relationship, is with yourself. Unfortunately, one thing that keeps people from getting in touch with their higher Self is a feeling of guilt, a feeling they're somehow not good enough. The greatest need in our soul is for us to achieve a complete loving of Self. It is impossible to feel the love of God if you do not love yourself because they are one and the same.

Guilt makes loving ourselves hard if not impossible. Guilt feelings manifest for various reasons but in the majority of cases guilt is accompanied by some form of addiction. Whether addiction manifests through drugs, alcohol, eating disorders, sex, or gambling, the addiction can be seen as a perverted form of searching for some measure of enlightenment or higher consciousness.

Addiction is caused by the perception that the particular substance or behavior somehow relieves emotional pain and/or gives pleasure. The addicted person is attempting to either avoid, enhance, or create certain states of feeling. It is imperative people address the underlying problem causing these symptoms in order to be successful at becoming the magnificent person they're meant to be.

One remedy for addiction, with a tremendously high

success rate, is EEG-Biofeedback Brain Wave Training. Alpha-theta brain wave training first appeared in the professional literature in 1989 when Dr. Gene Peniston published his work at a Department of Veterans Affairs hospital. In this study, 80% of those receiving neurofeedback training were able to quit drinking following a 30 day program. At the time of a 3 year follow-up the relapse rate was so low that the success figure declined by only 10%, a rate never before achieved.

If you or someone you love suffers with an addiction problem, you would do well to investigate a biofeedback program based on this principle. Resources for this therapy can be found in the back of this book.

To give you a simple overview of how this program works, understand that scientists identify four principle types of brain waves:

1). Beta is our normal waking state.
2). Alpha involves increased relaxation, when we have a sense of mindlessness.
3). Theta is experienced when we are very drowsy but not asleep.
4). Delta is dreamless sleep.

Through EEG biofeedback, one can learn to access the alpha/theta states. These psychophysiologic states then help people to not only overcome their addiction but they can also help set the stage for true enlightenment. Patients quickly learn through this training how to experience theta states of consciousness described as serene and peaceful. This provides them with many new abilities and possibilities. They develop a powerful coping skill; they realize that they have access to this inner calm no matter what is occurring in their environment. They realize that serenity is a present possibility and by learning to orient themselves to the particular Brainwave state associated with serenity, the individual gradually becomes free of the need for external things to provide relief. The stage is then set for the emergence of higher consciousness.

This is reiterated by Carl Jung who said, "If we understand and feel that here in this life we already have a link with the infinite, desires and attitudes change."

Some people, thinking it's a shortcut, resort to using mind-altering substances, supposedly to expand their consciousness. Doing drugs is akin to picking up a blind hitchhiker, putting him/her behind the wheel of your car, then jumping in the back seat to enjoy the ride. You're handing over control of your thoughts and actions to a substance capable only of doing harm. The devastating effects, the inevitable physical, psychological, and emotional addiction from abuse of any drug, gravely outweighs all perceived benefits.

Unlike drugs, enlightenment through meditation comes with just one side effect. Tapping into a universal consciousness, making a direct connection to God, will only cause your heart and soul to expand with love.

As stated earlier, one way to tap into your celestial library is through prayer and meditation. If prayer is talking to God, then meditation is listening to God talk to you. Meditation gives us a sense of calmness, clarity, and well being. It is essential in the search to discover who you really are as it allows you to deeply connect and attune your life with your true feelings. This in turn produces a tremendous inner contentment. Combined with prayer, it is a sure road to travel to obtain complete security and happiness. True security does not come from your job, your money, your family or friends. True security and joyful success comes from your ability to connect with the cosmic power of the Universe: God.

Meditation is best accomplished in 'down' time, when you are alone, everything is quiet and you will have no interruptions. Many people laugh and say that's impossible, they don't have time. Don't have time for God? That's a lame excuse. That's the same as saying you don't have time for your Self. Make the time. Aren't you worth it?

Spending quality time in solitude is the best investment you'll ever make. Steal time from sleep if necessary. Once you get the hang of meditating regularly, you'll find yourself thoroughly refreshed and able to exist on less sleep anyway so it's a great trade-off.

The importance of meditation is made clearer by comparing your mind to a bank account. If you continually write out checks without making any deposits you know what happens. You drain your account and wind up in debt. The same holds true with your mind and inner health. Each day of fighting battles, solving problems, just living life, uses up your supply of mental and emotional energy. If you don't replenish your psyche with calming and clarifying thoughts, you wind up depleted, feeling exhausted. Meditation is a sure fire way of building up your inner resolve to provide you with a reservoir of strength to fall back on.

Basically, the most simple instructions suffice when learning how to meditate. Use a relaxation technique (tighten then relax every muscle) to calm your body as you breathe deeply and gently from your lower abdomen. Lie down and place a book on your stomach. If it slowly rises and falls with each breath, you know you're breathing correctly. Empty the blackboard in your mind of all thoughts and problems. When one sneaks back in (and they will), grab the eraser and wipe it away. Center yourself, don't hesitate to ask God for help in doing so. Once you're relaxed, contemplate a loving image of God. Concentrate on Peace, Joy, Wisdom and Beauty. Simply open the door to your heart and soul and allow God's transcendent love to filter through.

The secret is really more in perseverance than method. Making the effort to practice meditation every day or nearly every day is the secret to success. You learn by doing and by doing you learn.

Daily prayer is also practiced by people living in the Luxury Suite. Particularly prayer for others. For every prayer request you send winging to God for yourself, send two for someone else.

Studies have shown there is no specific formula or dogma that results in one type of prayer being answered over another. And it makes no difference to God what religious denomination, if any, you belong to. As long as you're a member of the human race and you pray with sincerity, God hears you and loves you.

Of course prayer isn't always about asking or needing. Often it is a reflection of one's thanks for the little things in life, a simple way of expressing gratitude to God for another day, regardless of what happened in it.

Many people pray successfully when they pray for the

highest good for all concerned. The secret here is being willing and able to allow God to decide what that highest good is, not you. To accept whatever the outcome. To admit that God knows best.

As you look back over this book you can see we've come full circle. From reading about other people's synchronistic experiences to generating more of them in your own life by implementing a program of meditation and prayer.

Life holds many mysteries but coincidence is not one of them. If you thought all along that coincidence really is just God's way of remaining anonymous, I'd say you're absolutely correct.

Synchronicity is an intriguing, fascinating phenomenon. An earthly manifestation of God's love and caring.

For you. For me. For us all.

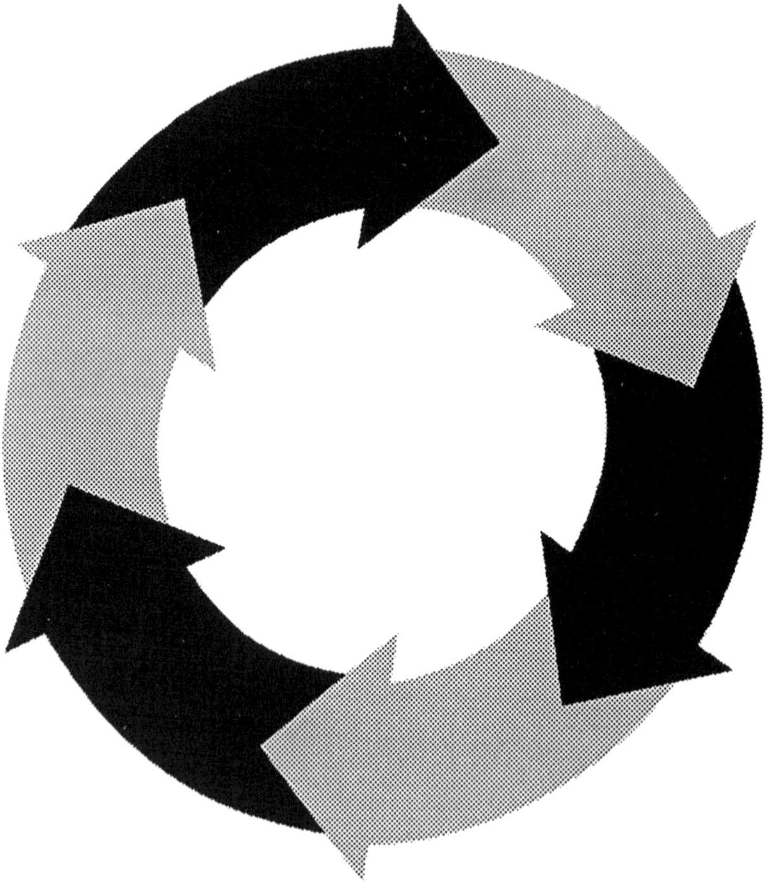

Chapter Six

A WORKBOOK FOR THE SOUL

The following philosophical exercise has no right or wrong answers. Simply be honest and write down what you feel.

To obtain insight into someone you love, remove Set B of the questions and give them to your partner. Both sets of questions are the same. Each person should answer the questions, writing your first answer as your own. Underneath your response, write what you think <u>your loved one will write</u> as his or her own answer. Compare results.

Know Thy Self

SET A

WHY DO YOU THINK YOU WERE BORN?

WHAT IS YOUR GREATEST STRENGTH?

WHAT IS YOUR GREATEST WEAKNESS?

TO DATE, WHAT DO YOU CONSIDER TO
BE YOUR GREATEST ACHIEVEMENT?

WHAT WILL IT BE
TEN YEARS FROM NOW?

**AT WHAT POINT IN YOUR LIFE,
SO FAR,
DID YOU FEEL HAPPIEST?**

**WHAT IS YOUR MOST PROFOUND
REGRET THAT YOU FEEL
YOU CAN YET RECTIFY?**

**WHAT IS YOUR MOST PROFOUND
REGRET YOU KNOW
YOU WILL NEVER RECTIFY?**

**IF, STARTING LIFE OVER,
YOU COULD LIVE TO BE 100, WITH YOUR
LAST 50 YEARS IN CHRONIC PAIN,
OR LIVE TO BE 50 IN PERFECT HEALTH,
WHICH WOULD YOU CHOOSE?**

OF ALL YOUR MATERIAL POSSESSIONS, WHICH DO YOU VALUE THE MOST?

IF YOU HAD TO START YOUR LIFE OVER, WOULD YOU CHOOSE TO BE THE SAME SEX?

*IF YOU COULD LIVE
ANYPLACE IN THE WORLD,
WHERE WOULD YOU LIVE AND WHY?*

WHAT ARE YOU MOST AFRAID OF?

***IF YOU HAD TO CHANGE PLACES
WITH SOMEONE YOU KNOW,
FOR ONE WEEK,
WHO WOULD IT BE AND WHY?***

***ARE YOU A NIGHT OWL
OR A
MORNING GLORY?***

*IF YOU COULD ASK GOD
ONE QUESTION,
WHAT WOULD IT BE?*

*IF YOU HAD TO CHOOSE
BETWEEN HAVING MONEY OR POWER
WHICH WOULD YOU CHOOSE?*

*IF YOU ONLY HAD ONE MONTH
BEFORE YOUR LIFE ON EARTH ENDED,
WHERE WOULD YOU GO,
WHAT WOULD YOU DO?*

*WHEN WAS THE LAST TIME YOU SAID
"I LOVE YOU" TO YOURSELF?*

*IS THERE ANYONE IN YOUR LIFE
YOU'D BE WILLING TO DIE FOR? WHO?*

*IF YOU HAD THE ABILITY TO FLY
OR THE ABILITY TO BE INVISIBLE
WHICH WOULD YOU CHOOSE AND WHY?*

*IF YOU COULD TALK FOR FIVE MINUTES
WITH SOMEONE YOU KNEW
PERSONALLY, WHO HAS DIED,
WHO WOULD IT BE?*

WOULD YOU RATHER EXCEL
(circle one)
ATHLETICALLY   INTELLECTUALLY   ARTISTICALLY

WHAT ASPECT OF YOUR PERSONALITY DO YOU FIND MOST APPEALING?

MOST UNAPPEALING?

WHAT IS YOUR GREATEST JOY IN LIFE?

YOU DEPEND ON YOUR SIXTH SENSE, INTUITION
(circle one)

ALWAYS   MOST OF THE TIME   OCCASIONALLY   NEVER

DO YOU AGREE OR DISAGREE WITH THE FOLLOWING STATEMENT AND EXPLAIN WHY YOU FEEL THE WAY YOU DO.

People who need people are the luckiest people in the world.

IF YOU WERE GOD WOULD YOU HAVE GIVEN MAN AND WOMAN FREE WILL? EXPLAIN WHY OR WHY NOT.

DESCRIBE YOUR RELATIONSHIP WITH GOD.

KNOW THY SELF

SET B

WHY DO YOU THINK YOU WERE BORN?

WHAT IS YOUR GREATEST STRENGTH?

WHAT IS YOUR GREATEST WEAKNESS?

*TO DATE, WHAT DO YOU CONSIDER TO
BE YOUR GREATEST ACHIEVEMENT?*

*WHAT WILL IT BE
TEN YEARS FROM NOW?*

*AT WHAT POINT IN YOUR LIFE,
SO FAR,
DID YOU FEEL HAPPIEST?*

*WHAT IS YOUR MOST PROFOUND
REGRET THAT YOU FEEL
YOU CAN YET RECTIFY?*

*WHAT IS YOUR MOST PROFOUND
REGRET YOU KNOW
YOU WILL NEVER RECTIFY?*

*IF, STARTING LIFE OVER,
YOU COULD LIVE TO BE 100, WITH YOUR
LAST 50 YEARS IN CHRONIC PAIN,
OR LIVE TO BE 50 IN PERFECT HEALTH,
WHICH WOULD YOU CHOOSE?*

OF ALL YOUR MATERIAL POSSESSIONS, WHICH DO YOU VALUE THE MOST?

IF YOU HAD TO START YOUR LIFE OVER, WOULD YOU CHOOSE TO BE THE SAME SEX?

***IF YOU COULD LIVE
ANYPLACE IN THE WORLD,
WHERE WOULD YOU LIVE AND WHY?***

WHAT ARE YOU MOST AFRAID OF?

*IF YOU HAD TO CHANGE PLACES
WITH SOMEONE YOU KNOW,
FOR ONE WEEK,
WHO WOULD IT BE AND WHY?*

*ARE YOU A NIGHT OWL
OR A
MORNING GLORY?*

*IF YOU COULD ASK GOD
ONE QUESTION,
WHAT WOULD IT BE?*

*IF YOU HAD TO CHOOSE
BETWEEN HAVING MONEY OR POWER
WHICH WOULD YOU CHOOSE?*

***IF YOU ONLY HAD ONE MONTH
BEFORE YOUR LIFE ON EARTH ENDED,
WHERE WOULD YOU GO,
WHAT WOULD YOU DO?***

***WHEN WAS THE LAST TIME YOU SAID
"I LOVE YOU" TO YOURSELF?***

***IS THERE ANYONE IN YOUR LIFE
YOU'D BE WILLING TO DIE FOR? WHO?***

**IF YOU HAD THE ABILITY TO FLY
OR THE ABILITY TO BE INVISIBLE
WHICH WOULD YOU CHOOSE AND WHY?**

**IF YOU COULD TALK FOR FIVE MINUTES
WITH SOMEONE YOU KNEW
PERSONALLY, WHO HAS DIED,
WHO WOULD IT BE?**

WOULD YOU RATHER EXCEL
(circle one)
ATHLETICALLY   INTELLECTUALLY   ARTISTICALLY

WHAT ASPECT OF YOUR PERSONALITY DO YOU FIND MOST APPEALING?

MOST UNAPPEALING?

WHAT IS YOUR GREATEST JOY IN LIFE?

YOU DEPEND ON YOUR SIXTH SENSE, INTUITION
(circle one)

ALWAYS   MOST OF THE TIME   OCCASIONALLY   NEVER

*DO YOU AGREE OR DISAGREE
WITH THE FOLLOWING STATEMENT
AND EXPLAIN WHY
YOU FEEL THE WAY YOU DO.*

P_{EOPLE} WHO NEED PEOPLE ARE THE LUCKIEST PEOPLE IN THE WORLD.

IF YOU WERE GOD
WOULD YOU HAVE GIVEN
MAN AND WOMAN FREE WILL?
EXPLAIN WHY OR WHY NOT.

DESCRIBE YOUR RELATIONSHIP WITH GOD.

****

If you have experienced an eventful,
synchronistic experience you'd like to share
for possible future publication,
please send it to the author at the address below.

Additional copies of this book
are available via mail.
Cost is $15.00 (12.00 + 3.00 shipping & postage)
for each book ordered.
Make check or money order payable to:
Universal Publications.

Universal Publications
P.O. Box 53511
Cincinnati, Ohio 45253

****

****

For additional information about EEG-Biofeedback Brain Wave Training, please contact:

Eugene Peniston, Ed.D.
Chief, Psychology Services
Sam Rayburn Memorial Veterans Center
1201 E. 9th Street
Bonham, Texas 75418-4091
(903) 583-2111

Dale Walters, Ph.D.
Sims-Kemper Clinical
Counseling & Recovery Services
1709 S.W. Medford
Topeka, Kansas 66604
(913) 233-0666 or 272-4678

****